DIWALI

By ALLAN MOREY

Illustrations by FLAVIA SORRENTINO

Music by MARK OBLINGER

CANTATA
LEARNING

WWW.CANTATALEARNING.COM

CANTATA LEARNING

Published by Cantata Learning
1710 Roe Crest Drive
North Mankato, MN 56003
www.cantatalearning.com

Library of Congress Cataloging-in-Publication Data
Names: Morey, Allan, author. | Sorrentino, Flavia, illustrator.
Title: Diwali / By Allan Morey ; Illustrations by Flavia Sorrentino ; Music
  by Mark Oblinger.
Description: North Mankato, MN : Cantata Learning, 2017. | Series: Holidays
  in Rhythm and Rhyme
Identifiers: LCCN 2017007568 (print) | LCCN 2017021011 (ebook) | ISBN
  9781684100224 | ISBN 9781684100217 (hardcover : alk. paper)
Subjects: LCSH: Divali--Juvenile literature.
Classification: LCC BL1239.82.D58 (ebook) | LCC BL1239.82.D58 M67 2017
  (print) | DDC 294.5/36--dc23
LC record available at https://lccn.loc.gov/2017007568

Book design, Tim Palin Creative
Editorial direction, Flat Sole Studio
Executive musical production and direction, Elizabeth Draper
Music arranged and produced by Mark Oblinger

Printed in the United States of America in North Mankato, Minnesota.
072017   0367CGF17

ACCESS THE MUSIC!

SCAN
CODE
WITH
MOBILE
APP

CANTATALEARNING.COM

TIPS TO SUPPORT LITERACY AT HOME

WHY READING AND SINGING WITH YOUR CHILD IS SO IMPORTANT

Daily reading with your child leads to increased academic achievement. Music and songs, specifically rhyming songs, are a fun and easy way to build early literacy and language development. Music skills correlate significantly with both phonological awareness and reading development. Singing helps build vocabulary and speech development. And reading and appreciating music together is a wonderful way to strengthen your relationship.

READ AND SING EVERY DAY!

TIPS FOR USING CANTATA LEARNING BOOKS AND SONGS DURING YOUR DAILY STORY TIME

1. As you sing and read, point out the different words on the page that rhyme. Suggest other words that rhyme.

2. Memorize simple rhymes such as Itsy Bitsy Spider and sing them together. This encourages comprehension skills and early literacy skills.

3. Use the questions in the back of each book to guide your singing and storytelling.

4. Read the included sheet music with your child while you listen to the song. How do the music notes correlate to the words of the song?

5. Sing along on the go and at home. Access music by scanning the QR code on each Cantata book. You can also stream or download the music for free to your computer, smartphone, or mobile device.

Devoting time to daily reading shows that you are available for your child. Together, you are building language, literacy, and listening skills.

Have fun reading and singing!

Diwali is also known as a **festival** of lights. This holiday lasts for five days and is celebrated in the fall. People light oil lamps called **diyas**, and there are also booming fireworks displays. Friends and family exchange gifts. They eat sweet treats and gather for holiday feasts.

To learn why Diwali is such a festive and colorful holiday, turn the page and sing along!

Hey, hey Diwali!
Happy Diwali!

Happy Diwali!
Diwali, hey, hey!

For five days and nights,
it's a festival of lights.

Clay diyas burn bright,
around the house at night.

Clean up your home so neat,
and put on new clothes head to feet.

10

Open doors and windows wide
to invite luck to come inside.

11

Hey, hey Diwali!
Happy Diwali!

Happy Diwali!
Diwali, hey, hey!

Draw **rangolis** on the ground,
swirling color all around.

Fireworks boom, oh, so loud.
Twirling sparklers all around.

Eat snacks and treats so sweet.
Have a great big family feast.

Give presents to your friends.
Let the joy never end!

Hey, hey Diwali!
Happy Diwali!

Happy Diwali!
Diwali, hey, hey!

Hey, hey Diwali!
Happy Diwali!

Happy Diwali!
Diwali, hey, hey!

SONG LYRICS
Diwali

Hey, hey, Diwali!
Happy Diwali!
Happy Diwali!
Diwali, hey, hey!

For five days and nights,
it's a festival of lights.
Clay diyas burn bright
around the house at night.

Clean up your home so neat,
and put on new clothes head to feet.
Open doors and windows wide
to invite luck to come inside.

Hey, hey, Diwali!
Happy Diwali!
Happy Diwali!
Diwali, hey, hey!

Draw rangolis on the ground,
swirling color all around.
Fireworks boom, oh, so loud.
Twirling sparklers all around.

Eat snacks and treats so sweet.
Have a great big family feast.
Give presents to your friends.
Let the joy never end!

Hey, hey, Diwali!
Happy Diwali!
Happy Diwali!
Diwali, hey, hey!

Hey, hey, Diwali!
Happy Diwali!
Happy Diwali!
Diwali, hey, hey!

Diwali

Holiday
Mark Oblinger

Chorus

Hey, hey, Di - wa - li! Hap - py Di - wa - li! Hap - py Di - wa - li! Di - wa - li, hey, hey!

Verse

1. For five days and nights, it's a fes - ti - val of lights. Clay di - yas burn bright a - round the house at night.

Verse 2
Clean up your home so neat,
and put on new clothes head to feet.
Open doors and windows wide
to invite luck to come inside.

Chorus

Verse 3
Draw rangolis on the ground,
swirling color all around.
Fireworks boom, oh, so loud.
Twirling sparklers all around.

Verse 4
Eat snacks and treats so sweet.
Have a great big family feast.
Give presents to your friends.
Let the joy never end!

Chorus

Outro

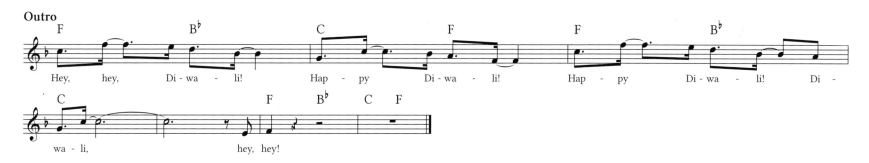

Hey, hey, Di - wa - li! Hap - py Di - wa - li! Hap - py Di - wa - li! Di - wa - li, hey, hey!

23

GLOSSARY

diyas—oil lamps used in India and Nepal

festival—a celebration or holiday

rangolis—colorful patterns that people create on a floor or on the ground outside using colored rice, colored sand, or flower petals

GUIDED READING ACTIVITIES

1. Rangolis are colorful designs that people create. Look at pages 12 and 13 for an example. Then draw your own rangolis.

2. People use oil lamps to decorate their homes for Diwali. Can you think of other holidays when people use special lighting to decorate?

3. Diwali is a time to enjoy treats with friends and family. What kinds of treats do you like? Do you have sweets on holidays? Which holidays?

TO LEARN MORE

Dickmann, Nancy. *Diwali*. Chicago: Heinemann Library, 2011.

Kenney, Karen Latchana. *Cool International Parties: Perfect Party Planning for Kids*. Minneapolis, MN: ABDO, 2012.

Murray, Julie. *Diwali*. Edina, MN: ABDO, 2014.

Pettiford, Rebecca. *Diwali*. Minneapolis: Bullfrog Books, 2015.